Excessively Blessed

DEVOTIONAL

Dr. Halene Giddens

ISBN: 978-1-7321277-2-2

FOR MORE INFORMATION CONTACT:
760-951-8500
www.destinychristiancenter.org

Cover art by Fred T. Williams Brand LLC

Acknowledgements

To my husband Bishop Jesse Giddens: your life has been a living epistle of God's holy presence and His goodness working in you and through you. Thank you for helping to lead me into the presence of the Lord.

To my beautiful spiritual parents in the faith, the late Apostle Nathaniel Holcomb and Pastor Valerie Holcomb: thank you for teaching me the beauty of staying in the Presence of the Lord.

To my Good Good Girlfriends (GGGF): thank you for believing I could do this! Thank you for encouraging me and helping me accept the truth that God has something to say to and through me.

Also, thank you to my beautiful sons and daughters in the Christian faith who prayed, prophesied, and helped push this work to the finish. May our Heavenly Father continue to bless the work of your hands and the gift of your heart.

To my God: You invited me to not just pause in Your Presence but have also enticed me to dwell right where You are all of the days of my life. Thank you, Lord Jesus!

Dr. Halene Giddens

A NOTE FROM DR. HALENE

Pause in His Presence

God, you're such a safe and powerful place to find refuge!
You're a proven help in time of trouble —
more than enough and always available whenever I need you.
So we will never fear even if every structure of support
were to crumble away. We will not fear even when
the earth quakes and shakes, moving mountains
and casting them into the sea. For the raging roar of
stormy winds and crashing waves
cannot erode our faith in you.
Pause in his presence.

Psalms 46:1-3 TPT

Dr. Halene Giddens

God bless you! I pray that you are excessively blessed today and that God's favor rests upon you and your entire household. The Word of God says in Psalm 31:15, "Our times are in His hands." That means whatever season we are in, our Heavenly Father is lifting us; so be assured that you are in the best care.

There may be times in our lives when it may look as though God is not with us or has left us. Our world is filled with tragedy, catastrophic events, devastating losses, and unexplained disasters, yet we, as believers, have hope. Acknowledging that we have hope caused me to search the Word to see what He has to say, and Psalm 46 speaks clearly about His position: God is on our side. We have the Maker of the universe always available whenever we need Him! He clearly states His position with us, but it's up to us to seek, trust, and believe in Him.

The end of Psalm 46 in the Passion Translation advises us

Halene Giddens

to "Pause in his presence." The King James Version interprets this with Selah: a place of waiting, taking a moment to be quiet and still. We are to live our lives taking moments to pause in the presence of the Lord. We should seek God's presence, especially when the issues of life become overwhelming around us. This is when we need that pause break.

As we purposely take this pause, let's give our worries over to our God, letting the fear cease to taunt us and the doubt halt because we are in the presence of the Almighty. God is our present help, our Sovereign Savior Who we can trust with our every concern and care. Just as I noted at the beginning of today's devotional, He holds our future in His hands. He is a safe and powerful place in which we find refuge! As we pause in His presence, know that He is always present with us. Always!

The Lord is more than enough for us, and He is readily available whenever we need Him. In the midst of calamity, chaos, and crisis, our God is a powerful place to find refuge. Any time

Halene Giddens

is the right time to give Him all the glory and praise, keeping our eyes uplifted, our hands outstretched, and our hearts turned toward Him! Let's always find the time and the space to pause in His presence. He is on our side! May God continue to bless you, and may His anointing fall fresh upon you today. Amen!

Halene Giddens

O N E

Comfort and Strength in the Word

Wait on the Lord: be of good courage, and he shall strengthen thine heart: wait, I say, on the Lord.

Psalm 27:14 KJV

If troubles weigh us down, that just means that we will receive even more comfort to pass on to you for your deliverance! For the comfort pouring into us empowers us to bring comfort to you. And with this comfort upholding you, you can endure victoriously the same suffering that we experience.

2 Corinthians 1:6 TPT

Dr. Halene Giddens

I pray you are doing well on this blessed day! I pray that you experience God's peace as you go throughout your day. I pray that this Word will cause you to pause in His presence and welcome Him in to fill you up with His Spirit.

Today, I would like to share two verses of Scripture. First, in Psalm 27, King David encourages us that the Word has the ability to give us strength in any situation, no matter what we are going through. God's Word can comfort us. Allow this passage to invigorate and boost you. Second, as the body of Christ, we are called to have a close and intimate relationship with Jesus. Our Heavenly Father desires that we diligently seek His heart in every matter. He loves us and only has our best interest at heart.

The Apostle Paul wrote the book of Corinthians to the church of Corinth, and here, just as David did in Psalms, Paul urges us that if we are troubled, filled with anxiety, or concerned about our future, we can receive God's comfort. However, Paul takes

Halene Giddens

it one step further, telling us that just as the Father consoles us with His love and peace, we have the capability of sharing this gift with others.

His comfort is what assures our faith that when we allow the Father's love to fill us and share it with others, we are strengthened in the process. When we allow ourselves to dwell in His presence, we can bring peace and contentment to every person we meet and in every situation brought before us. God bless you today and be comforted by His Word.

Halene Giddens

T W O

God is a Strong Tower

But I will sing of Your mighty strength and power;
yes, I will sing aloud of Your mercy and loving-kindness
in the morning; for You have been to me a defense
(a fortress and a high tower)
and a refuge in the day of my distress.
Unto You, O my Strength, I will sing praises;
for God is my Defense, my Fortress, and High Tower,
the God Who shows me mercy and steadfast love.
Psalm 59:16-17 AMPC

Dr. Halene Giddens

G ood day to you! I pray you are doing well and resting in God's presence. As I meditate on God's goodness even amid tragedy, I am reminded of this Psalm and allow it to settle in my heart to bring me His peace. I hope it speaks to you as well.

This poetic composition proclaims to us that our God is a strong tower; He is our defense, a fortress that we can run into and find safety. Jesus Christ, our Lord, Savior, and soon coming King, is our protector. He will be our refuge and will vindicate us.

So many worries may plague your heart and mind, but you can, right now in your private moment, lift up a song of praise and worship to your God and sing of His mighty strength and power! Jesus is your strength, and He will get you through the tough times. Enemies may be trying to come against you, but let Him be your deliverer and defense. Run into the security of His love and let Him be your safe place of peace.

Halene Giddens

Remember that our God is merciful. In the book of Lamentations, Jeremiah tells us that "Every morning, His mercies are new to us." Allow yourself to be refreshed in God's peaceful presence. Take it with you throughout the day and call upon Him, allowing Him to be your strength. If you feel anxious, scared, or are having a moment of uncertainty, recall these verses and meditate on them. Sing to yourself, telling yourself that He is your peace, and you are free to run into the fortress of His arms.

I pray that you receive the strength He has for you today. I pray that you will sing of the goodness of the Lord forever! It doesn't matter what you sound like, just sing! Your singing is a defense against the onslaught of the enemy. So, let the melodies of the Lord arise in your heart and sing songs of deliverance! Our God is a Mighty Fortress Who protects you from harm. God bless you today.

Halene Giddens

T H R E E

Be Well Today

*People everywhere seem to worry
about making a living,
but your heavenly Father knows your every need
and will take care of you.
As you passionately seek his kingdom,
above all else, he will supply your needs.
So don't ever be afraid, dearest friends!
Your loving Father joyously gives you his kingdom
with all its promises!*

Luke 12:30-32 TPT

Dr. Halene Giddens

I pray that you are well mentally, emotionally, physically, spiritually and receiving healing and wellness in every area of your life.

The Gospels of Luke and Matthew both record Jesus telling us that we should take no thought of what we should wear, eat, drink, or any of these things. At this time, Jesus introduces God as our Father and tells us that He knows everything we need and will take care of us.

This passage is precluded by Luke 12:13, where Jesus is walking and teaching among the crowds gathered around Him. A man yells to Him, "Master, you should compel my older brother to divide the family inheritance and give me my fair share!" Jesus' response is what brings about His teaching for us to "take no thought." He tells the man, "Who made me a judge or arbitrator over you?" In essence, Jesus is telling us that the least of things are earthly riches; we need to concern ourselves with our heavenly inheritance instead.

Halene Giddens

Jesus encourages us in Luke 12:30-32 that God desires to give us everything that pertains to the Kingdom of God. It is profound that our Heavenly Father wants to give us the Kingdom: not only what is in the Kingdom but also the Kingdom itself and all that is connected to it.

It may be difficult to conceptualize how to have a Kingdom mindset and not worry about the cares of this world, yet our Father desires for us to pursue Him passionately. In our pursuit of Him, He promises to give us the right to rule and reign with authority in this life! That means with every challenge we face, we will overcome and obtain victory!

As we cast aside our desires and lean not on our own understanding, we can have the kingdom mindset, which produces kingdom dominion. God's Kingdom is above every principality, every problem, and all outside evil attacks. We must see our lives now and in our future from the kingdom vantage point, high above the fray! Allow God to show you how He

Halene Giddens

sees you in your situation, reigning and ruling as kings! The Kingdom will be yours as you seek first the King! Be passionate in your pursuit to seek Him first with all your heart.

Halene Giddens

F O U R

Hope Today

But then I choose to remember God, and this is my hope:
The Lord's love never comes to an end.
He never stops being kind to us.
Every day, we can trust him to be kind again.
We know that he will do what he has promised to do.
'He is my Lord,' I say to myself. '
He is the reason why I can hope for good things.'
The Lord does good things for people who wait for him.
He is kind to everyone who looks for him.
It is good when people continue to hope.
It is good when they quietly wait for the Lord,
because he will save them. It is also good for people to obey God
when they are young. They should work well for him.

Lamentations 3: 21-27 EEB

Dr. Halene Giddens

This is the day that the Lord has made! Let us choose to rejoice and be glad in it! I pray that you are speaking hope into every area concerning your life for your words have power. In every aspect of your life where there is lack, you have authority to prevail, given by the Father. You just have to say the Word.

I would like to share this passage in Lamentations, written by the prophet Jeremiah. Also known as the Weeping Prophet, he cries out to God on behalf of the children of Israel due to the horrible circumstances they were in. I pray that these verses uplift you and help you know that your hope is always in your God. Even when our situation seems bleak and discouraging, we must choose to remember to keep our hope in God.

The prophet Jeremiah is reminding us that our God is a kind God. His steadfast love for us is never-ending. Therefore, it is good for us to trust and obey the Lord, always looking to Him. Child of God, it is good for us to patiently wait in expectation

Halene Giddens

for Him to rescue, deliver, heal, and give us a future full of His unlimited blessings. As you look to the Lord and believe in Him concerning your faith, family, finances, and future, remind yourself of the victory He promises, which is precisely what Jeremiah did. Choose to trust Him with your life and believe you will see the salvation of the Lord. That is a promise He will keep. No matter what you face, if your hope is in your God, He will be with you and bring you out!

Halene Giddens

FIVE

David's Complaint

"I cry out to the Lord with my voice;
With my voice to the Lord I make my supplication.
I pour out my complaint before Him;
I declare before Him my trouble.
I cried out to You, O Lord;
I said, "You are my refuge,
My portion in the land of the living."

Psalm 142:1-2, 5 NKJV

Dr. Halene Giddens

How are you today? I pray you're doing exceptionally well and will continue to walk in God's wellness for your life. As I was looking in the Word of God, I noticed the patriarchs and matriarchs of old who made their complaint to the Lord! Imagine my surprise when I discovered in the Scriptures that people complained to God! Job complained! In the book of Lamentations, Jeremiah cried out with his complaint before the Lord, and here we see King David pouring his complaint out before his God!

I have heard many declare that there is no use in complaining; I have even said it myself. We are even encouraged to stop complaining. However, the Word displays people, like you and me, in distress complaining to God. We know of Hannah's complaint to the Lord concerning her barren womb. Leah complained of an unloving husband.

These Scriptures in Psalm 142 show us that King David presented his complaint before the Lord. He faced several issues

Halene Giddens

and had several urgent matters coming against him. You, like David, may be challenged by circumstances outside of your control. You may be under physical attack within your body, a spiritual attack with your family, disagreement with friends, or in a financial crisis; whatever the case, you may feel you have a legitimate cause to complain. Make your complaint, cry out before your God and receive Him as your present help. God really will be right there.

King David said, "God, You are my portion. You are my refuge. You are the One that rescues me." Trust that God will rescue you because He hears your complaint. Turn your complaint and your cry before the Lord into praise, and let your trouble be turned into triumph!

Remember, no matter your complaint, whatever your issue is, you can cry out before your God regardless of what you are going through. He hears you. He will help you. Wait for Him patiently. As Jeremiah proclaimed, "I waited quietly and

Halene Giddens

patiently before the Lord." When you make your complaint to the Lord, allow your heart to receive His correction and direction for your situation. Make sure to declare His goodness and rehearse His promises even when you don't see them quite yet. He'll meet you where you are as you cry out to Him! So, before you complain to anyone else, make your complaint to the Lord and leave it right there. Have an excessively blessed day today!

Halene Giddens

SIX

Safely in His Sanctuary

In your day of danger
may Yahweh answer and deliver you.
May the name of the God of Jacob
set you safely on high!
May supernatural help be sent
from his sanctuary.
May he support you
from Zion's fortress!
Psalm 20:1-2 TPT

Dr. Halene Giddens

Praise the Lord! God bless you! I pray you experience God's healing hand of hope and help today. Psalm 20 encourages us to find supernatural help from God's Holy Sanctuary. This passage of Scripture teaches us that Yahweh will answer and deliver us when we call on Him. When we call on the Name of God, He will set us in a safe place in dangerous circumstances.

This particular passage in the Passion Translation says, "May he support you from Zion's fortress." We receive the undergirding support we need just by being in the strong and mighty fortress found in Zion, the Sanctuary of the Lord. The very answers that you need can come just by entering the Sanctuary. Yahweh speaks in the midst of His people, especially in joint worship and praise.

In the book of Genesis, also known as the Book of Beginnings, Moses discovered that God is Who He is, everything and all things, one of the many translations of God's Name Yahweh.

Halene Giddens

God wants to be everything and all that we need. He wants to show us aspects of Who He is in our everyday lives when we call to Him.

We also can recognize our hearts should be settled in Him because we find peace by fellowshipping with Him. To confirm this, we find in Revelations 21:3, "Behold, the tabernacle of God is with men." We are the living sanctuary of the Lord. Therefore, we allow Him to infiltrate our hearts as we meditate on the goodness and greatness of His Word, allowing Him to permeate our hearts and minds.

As you continue to read this chapter in the book of Psalms, you learn that He will remember every gift that we give unto Him. He will not forget all our giving nor fail to recall our sacrificial offerings to the House of God. In His generosity, God also puts gifts within us for His glory to be a blessing to those around us.

Halene Giddens

Be at peace as you fellowship with your God! Remember that God is your present help, and He will give you His victory. Rely on Him, depend on Him, and trust in Him. Consequently, if you find yourself in danger, God is your help and strength. Call on the Name of Yahweh; He desires you to receive His full support in every area and season of your life!

Halene Giddens

S E V E N

God's Presence

*And they heard the voice of the Lord God
walking in the garden in the cool of the day:
and Adam and his wife hid themselves
from the presence of the Lord God
amongst the trees of the garden.*

Genesis 3:8 KJV

Dr. Halene Giddens

I pray you're doing well today! I pray that you are excessively and abundantly blessed. What a blessing it is to live this life with God's presence always with us! I pray that's where you find yourself right now, enjoying God's presence right there where you are.

Today I want to visit the first time the presence of God is mentioned in the Word. It should have been a wondrous and momentous occasion, one filled with glory and delight. But unfortunately, the first time God's presence is introduced is when Adam and Eve are trying to hide from Him. It's heartbreaking to think that anyone would want to hide from the presence of the Lord!

When we pursue after someone, it's typically someone that we care for and love. We look to spend time with them and desire to enjoy their company. We seek to deepen our relationship and simply live our lives together. God wants the same thing with us. He is constantly pursuing us, and it devastates Him when we try

Halene Giddens

to hide from Him. It breaks His heart when we turn our sights toward someone or something else. Yet, He still comes after us.

The beauty in this verse is that God already knew that Adam and Eve had sinned, and He sought them anyway. God still wanted to spend time with His son and daughter, but they hid because of their guilt and shame when they heard their Father's voice.

Child of God, I pray that as you go through your day that you hear our Father's voice. Listen for His footsteps and run toward Him. Don't hide; fall at His feet as the Syrophoenician woman did and worship Him there. Do not allow sin, guilt, or shame to keep you from His presence. He is walking toward you, pursuing you. Hear Him call for you, and like a child, run to Him with open arms.

May God keep you, cover you, watch over you, and bless you excessively in every aspect and area of your life today and

Halene Giddens

always!

Halene Giddens

E I G H T

A Prayer of Confidence

"Protect me, O God; I trust in you for safety.
I say to the Lord, "You are my Lord;
all the good things I have come from you."
You, Lord, are all I have,
and you give me all I need;
my future is in your hands.
How wonderful are your gifts to me;
how good they are!"

Psalm 16:1-2, 5-6 GNT

Dr. Halene Giddens

I pray that you are excessively blessed and expecting great success today! This is the day that the Lord has made, and He desires you to rejoice in this truth before you start on your day. I hope that Psalm 16 encourages you to live out the life that God has for you despite any negative report that may come your way.

Psalm 16 is called "A Prayer of Confidence." To be confident is to be reliant upon something or someone. It also means to have faith in or to be assured of a person or thing. In essence, this short chapter in this sacred Book of Psalms is compelling us to rely on the protection and safety of our Lord.

It seems almost impossible because we can't see Him in this physical realm. Yet, this is why we must believe and know in the spiritual realm that He is ever-present with us. David lived this way, and we know this because, in verse eight, he wrote, "I am always aware of the Lord's presence; he is near, and nothing can shake me." This confidence that David had concerning the

Halene Giddens

presence of the Lord is the same confidence we can have. We should always be aware of our Father's presence; we shouldn't allow anything to shake us from Him.

As we dwell in His wraparound presence every moment, we are made confident of His safe keeping. Then, we can possess a newfound level of security. We can believe in healing and freedom for ourselves and those around us. We can rest in knowing that because we choose to dwell in His presence, inside the fortress that He is, He will watch over our every care and take on to Himself the burdens that weigh us down.

Tell the Lord He's all you need. Everything good comes from Him. Allow Him to be your security. He desires us to look to Him in every situation and be at peace because we are confident that He makes all things work together for our good. Believe this for your life today! God bless you, and I love you!

Halene Giddens

NINE

The Invitation

"Are you weary, carrying a heavy burden?
Then come to me.
I will refresh your life, for I am your oasis.
Simply join your life with mine.
Learn my ways, and you'll discover that
I'm gentle, humble, easy to please.
You will find refreshment and rest in me.
For all that I require of you will be pleasant and easy to bear."

Matthew 11:28-30 TPT

Dr. Halene Giddens

Praise the Lord. I pray you are blessed exceedingly, abundantly, and above all, you can even ask or think today. I pray you take the time to have sweet communion and fellowship with the Lord. Right where you are, if you can, take a moment to meditate on the Lord, worship Him, and love on Him. Think only of Him, all that He is, and all that He has done. I believe that during this time, this break in your busy schedule, He will strengthen you and shower you with His love.

This mindset brings me to this passage in Matthew. These verses are extra special because these words are straight from Jesus' lips. Jesus is conversing with His Heavenly Father out loud for all to hear. He is telling us longingly and lovingly to rest in Him. He is letting us know that His desire is for us to join our lives with His. To join means connecting, attaching, or fusing together, which is what He wants us to do!

Oh, that we would grab ahold of the promise that Jesus wants to carry our heavy burdens! He doesn't want us to worry

Halene Giddens

or fret. Our Lord wants to be our oasis, our place of serenity and peace. He doesn't want us to concern ourselves with how He will work everything out for our good. He simply wants us to attach our lives to His. He promises us that He is "gentle, humble, and easy to please." I love that about our Lord and Savior!

I pray that you join yourself with our Lord Jesus, allowing Him to carry every weight. Make the choice today to run to Him with every concern, complaint, and issue. He will uplift, strengthen, and refresh you. Receive His peace that passes all our understanding. Trust that your Father in Heaven knows what's best for your life and receive this invitation to let Him carry your every worry.

As you continue throughout your day, remember the time you took to release your burdens and cares to your Heavenly Father. Because He's refreshed you as you've joined your life with His, walk in His strength, peace, and joy. God bless you! I

Halene Giddens

pray that you stay refreshed in His Word always.

Halene Giddens

TEN

The Shema

Hear, O Israel:
The LORD our God is one LORD:
and thou shalt love the LORD thy God
with all thine heart,
and with all thy soul,
and with all thy might.

Deuteronomy 6:4-5 KJV

Dr. Halene Giddens

I pray this Word from God brings you comfort and clarity concerning your life. I hope that you will be found in His perfect peace in whatever you may face today. Let this Word reassure you of His promise.

This passage of Scripture, written by the hand of Moses, is part of the Shema, which is the affirmation of the Singularity of God, His Oneness, His Wholeness. The *Shema*, which also means *to herald or hear with clarity*, is traditionally what the Jewish people proclaim twice every day. They declare the Sovereignty of God every morning and evening as part of their daily prayers. Moses taught them to do this long ago. He stressed that the children of Israel teach their children this commandment: to love the Lord with all your heart, soul, mind, and strength.

This command is not only for our Jewish brothers and sisters but also for all believers. Jesus makes this clear in Matthew 22:37. Then in verse 38, He tells us that this is the first and greatest commandment.

Halene Giddens

To love the Lord with our whole heart means to make Him the focal point of our lives. Just as our heart is found at the center of our chest, Christ should be found at the center, or heart, of our lives. This means that we love God wholeheartedly no matter what is happening around us; He is our center.

To love the Lord our God with all our soul is loving Him with all we have and all we think. We must place the things we hold so dearly in His hands, like our family, loved ones, and anything we consider valuable. When we love Him with all our soul, we give everything over to Him. Essentially, all that He has given us, we give right back to Him.

As we love the Lord with all our minds, we release the cares and concerns that plague our minds daily. When we read and think about His healing Word, we allow those words to soothe our weary minds. We can have success every day when our minds are cleared from the constant clutter of our clouded thoughts.

Halene Giddens

Loving the Lord our God with all our might means letting go of our strength. Allowing Him to take our gifts, talents, and treasures releases us from the burden of competition and comparison. When we give Him back the abilities He put within us, we allow Him to use them for His intended purposes.

As you go throughout your day, remember the Shema. Recite it over your life. Teach it to your family. Declare, "Lord, I love You above everything else!" As you place Him first in every area of your life—-with all your heart, soul, mind, and strength—you will learn to align your wants to His; He will answer the desires of your heart. Commit your life, heart, family, and all that encompasses your world to Him, and you will receive all that you need and desire! God bless you, Saints of the Most High God! I pray that you will be excessively blessed today!

Halene Giddens

E L E V E N

God Works Everything Out For Our Good

And we know that all things
work together
for good to them
that love God,
to them who are the called
according to his purpose.

Romans 8:28 KJV

Dr. Halene Giddens

God bless you, beloved! My hope for you today is that God is your priority because I guarantee you are His priority. His banner over you is love, and He is always with you.

Romans 8:28 has always been a part of my confession over my life. I read this verse daily and profess it as it encourages and gives me renewed strength. I pray it does the same for you.

We are unsure what our future holds or how our circumstances may change, yet even in this, we can know Who holds our future. Every day, we face a new set of decisions to make: a choice to live a life fully with Him or a life in darkness without His guidance and care. Every day we must choose. Thus, I confess this Word daily to remind myself that I am promised that all things work together for my good even in hardship or tragedy. You can apply this same vow to your life. Make it personal. Tell God that you love Him; tell Him that you give Him your life and all that you hold dear. You are His child,

Halene Giddens

and He only has the best in store for you.

All of us who name Jesus Christ as our Lord and Savior are called according to His divine purpose. Romans 8:29 goes on to tell us that we are predestined and preordained. This means that we share the same DNA as Jesus; we are in His family! We are set apart for His purpose and glory! We are His.

What joy we have! Though we face hardship, tests, and trials just like our Lord and Savior, we are set aside to do great things in His Name! We are made for this! We have been justified, glorified, and set aside on purpose with purpose. He will surely work out anything that comes against us for our good!

I pray, child of God, that you keep this in your mind, and whatever you face today, this week, or this month, believe that He is working it all out for your good because you love Him, and you're called to be with Him! You will have a testimony after it! God bless you and have a favorable day!

Halene Giddens

Pause in His Presence

T W E L V E

Our God Fulfills His Promise

"You are the Lord God, Who chose Abram
And brought him out of Ur of the Chaldees,
And gave him the name Abraham.
"You found his heart to be faithful before You,
And You made a covenant with him
To give him the land of the Canaanite, of the Hittite,
of the Amorite, of the Perizzite, the Jebusite, and the Girgashite —
To give it to his descendants. And You have fulfilled Your promise,
For You are righteous and just.

Nehemiah 9:7-8 AMP

Dr. Halene Giddens

Praise the Lord beloved saint of the Most High God! I pray this day finds you excessively blessed! I pray that the Holy Spirit on the inside of you strengthens you with His love.

Many say that America is a Christian nation, and although Christians live here, America as a whole does not necessarily embrace Christian values. As a whole, our nation does not put God first, just as it was in the days of Nehemiah. God was not their main priority. Though Nehemiah was born in captivity and served the king of Persia as his cupbearer, he desired to rebuild the Temple of God located in Jerusalem.

Nehemiah, whose name happens to mean Jehovah comforts, heard of the dilapidated walls in the city, and the news grieved his heart. The Temple was destroyed due to war and the capture of the Israelites. The Israelites, called God's chosen, did not choose to serve God. They sinned against Him over and over again. They refused to do what was right and pleasing in His

Halene Giddens

sight, and as a result, He allowed them to be taken into bondage. I thank God that we are under His mercy and grace in today's dispensation. Yet, we can still allow our sin issues along with guilt and shame to bind and control us, leaving us captive.

Here we see Nehemiah reminding God of the promise He made to Abraham. Today, God still desires to fulfill every promise concerning you. You may be like Nehemiah, having to ask permission from someone higher than you to do God's will. But remember, like Nehemiah, you serve a God Who is just and righteous. He has a promise that He wants to fulfill through you.

In these verses of Scripture, Nehemiah thanked God for the promise He made and kept! Because Nehemiah's heart was toward God, he found favor with the king as a slave in a foreign nation. Nehemiah received this favor so he could fulfill the will of God, not just for his life, but for the nation of Israel.

Though we live in a nation that does not acknowledge God

Halene Giddens

as its Sovereign and Supreme Ruler, we can pray for our country and watch God fulfill His promise concerning His children that dwell here. Repeat these words of Nehemiah: "You, oh God, have fulfilled Your promise, for you Lord are righteous and just." I pray that you would go after every promise He has for you to receive and fulfill! I love you! May you experience the joy of the Lord as your strength today.

Halene Giddens

T H I R T E E N

The Blessing of The Benediction

Now may the God of peace [the source of serenity and spiritual well-being] who brought up from the dead our Lord Jesus, the great Shepherd of the sheep, through the blood that sealed and ratified the eternal covenant, equip you with every good thing to carry out His will and strengthen you [making you complete and perfect as you ought to be], accomplishing in us that which is pleasing in His sight, through Jesus Christ, to whom be the glory forever and ever. Amen.

Hebrews 13:20-21 AMP

Dr. Halene Giddens

Praise the Lord! May you walk in the amazing manifold blessings of the Lord today! May you sense God's peace and His presence with you throughout your day. He wants you to live the most fulfilling life on this side of Heaven! So, reach out and receive it!

Though there is no ascribed writer for the book of Hebrews, it's often attributed to the Apostle Paul. He may have decided not to identify himself in this letter because he and others alongside him were called to the Gentiles to preach the Gospel of Jesus Christ. Instead, God called the Apostle Peter along with the brothers of Jesus and others to the Hebrew people. Whomever the author may have been, his desire was for the church to be strengthened to accomplish the will of God. The author tells us to commit and submit ourselves to walk in the purpose God has called us to live.

We are here to do His will. Let that sink in. We are not here for ourselves, but we are here for Him. This is the reason

Halene Giddens

we were created. He promises that He will strengthen us to do all He's anointed and appointed us to do. He will take care of everything we choose to give to Him. He will take care of our family, jobs, and future; we just need to give them to Him every day. As we let go and commit our hearts, minds, and will to His, God will use us for His glory and His purpose.

This passage promises that as we trust Him and give Him license to take over, He will make us complete and perfect just as we ought to be. We will be pleasing in His sight when we give our lives over to Him and let Him accomplish the perfect work He has planned for our lives. When we desire God's peace and allow His power to flow through us, we please Him.

As you submit yourself and commit your ways to God, He will strengthen you to do all He has called you to do. I pray that you follow His guidance and leading as He is the Source of your serenity and spiritual well-being. Let the Holy Spirit show you His will for your life, allowing Him to make you complete and

Halene Giddens

perfect in Him. In this, you will always be pleased to dwell with Him. Be blessed today!

Halene Giddens

Pause in His Presence

F O U R T E E N

Offering Our Praise to The Most High God

*Blessed be the Lord, Who daily loadeth us with benefits,
even the God of our salvation. Selah*

Psalm 68:19 KJV

*I will offer all my loving praise to you,
and I thank you so much for answering my prayer
and bringing me salvation!*

Psalm 118:21 TPT

Dr. Halene Giddens

God bless you today! I pray that you are in expectation of seeing every benefit, blessing, and bonus the Lord has for you. He woke you up this morning with a purpose and a plan. So, receive the abundance and security He so freely offers you.

We all can have moments and sometimes days that cause us to have questions or make us complain. People in the Word of God have cried out to protest what was happening to them. Yet, we must grab hold of this truth, right in the middle of our circumstance: God is the One Who sees you through the trying times. The challenging situations in our lives are not for our destruction but can be used for our perfection. If we allow Him, God, through the Holy Spirit, uses challenges to strengthen our faith in Him and for us to come to know Him more intimately. Without the downs, we wouldn't appreciate the ups. Without the tests, we wouldn't have the testimony.

These verses of the Bible bring great hope. David had

Halene Giddens

many tests, trials, death threats, and tragedies in his life. Some situations he put himself in and other problems he faced weren't his fault at all. However, in every circumstance, David had an unwavering faith in God. Despite everything David went through, he still offered loving praises and blessings to the Lord. I believe because of all that David went through—things that would make most people crumble and faint—his relationship with the Lord only deepened and became more solid. David's determination in all things was to offer all his loving praise to his Father. He truly was a man after God's heart.

Let the blessings of the Lord ever be on your lips. Confess them and declare them over your life every day! He daily loads you down with the benefit of life, hope, help, and healing. Don't ever forget that we are running the race for the glory of God. He will bring you out of every dark situation brighter than when you went in! So, continue to give Him your ultimate praise! God bless you!

Halene Giddens

F I F T E E N

God's Divine Presence

"I thank you, Lord, and with all the passion of my heart
I worship you in the presence of angels!
Heaven's mighty ones will hear my voice
as I sing my loving praise to you.
I bow down before your divine presence and bring you my deepest
worship as I experience your tender love and your living truth.
For your Word and the fame of your name
have been magnified above all else!
You keep every promise you've ever made to me!
Since your love for me is constant and endless, I ask you, Lord,
to finish every good thing that you've begun in me!"

Psalm 138:1-2, 8 TPT

Dr. Halene Giddens

Blessings to you today! I pray this day finds you walking in the presence of God and in the fullness of His favor. I pray that you personalize and internalize today's Psalm and know the total sum of the love God has for you.

Psalm 138 is a beautiful song that King David sang unto the Lord entitled "The Divine Presence" in the Passion Translation. This Psalm shows the posture that David takes in worshipping our Lord. David says that with all the passion of his heart, he worships in the presence of the angels and that Heaven's mighty ones will hear him as he sings praises! He bows before the Lord, bringing his deepest worship unto God.

We should follow David's example and praise out loud the Lord our God, bowing down in His presence. Give thanks freely and joyfully, for it's by His mighty power that you make it through any devastation and are revived! Remember, and even speak with boldness, all that He has done for you, all that He has brought you through, the many blessings He bestowed upon

Halene Giddens

you, and lift it to Him with thanksgiving and praise.

Let the words of this Psalm become yours, spoken sincerely as your heart's desire. Let this Psalm be praise from your heart to our Lord! Remind Him of the words of assurance that He's spoken to you. Tell Him how He has vowed to keep every promise He made you. Rely on the Word of God every day for your livelihood. Don't forget His commands. Try not to concern yourself with how long it may take to see His promises manifest in the physical realm. Simply believe and know that He is working it all out in the spiritual realm.

May you trust His infallible promises and greatness to accomplish these precious promises for you! He desires to do these things for you. May His goodness toward you be magnified today! Continually thank Him for all His benefits, bonuses, and blessings He bestows upon you daily.

Thank Him for allowing you to see another day and let His

Halene Giddens

peaceful presence be with you. Love on your Heavenly Father today and be excessively blessed!

Halene Giddens

SIXTEEN

Receive the Wisdom of God

Say unto wisdom,
Thou art my sister;
and call understanding
thy kinswoman
Proverb 7:4 KJV

Dr. Halene Giddens

I pray this day finds you receiving the greatest of blessings from God. I pray He gives you the knowledge and wisdom you need in every area and in all situations you may find yourself in today. Seek His wisdom, and He will freely give it to you.

The book of Proverbs is the wisdom book. We learn wisdom was there with God at the Creation of all things, and that wisdom calls out to us, wanting us to follow after her. In Proverbs 7:4, Solomon, the wisest man who has ever lived and the author of Proverbs, encourages us to call wisdom our sister and treat her as a close relative. We should treat wisdom just like we would trust our best friend. King Solomon is pleading with us to always entrust the wisdom of God, in everything.

King Solomon advises that when we lean on and give all our confidence to God and His infinite wisdom, He will take us to a place of peace and comfort. Acknowledging God in all our ways and granting Him access to every hidden area we want

Halene Giddens

65

to work out ourselves allows Him to direct and straighten the path before us. The wisdom of God relieves us of all anxiety and gives us strength.

God desires for you to receive His wisdom. He hopes that every decision you make has wisdom applied to it. Wisdom will direct you and show you where to go. Wisdom will prosper every road you find yourself on. Making wisdom your closest friend allows God to use you as a vessel of knowledge and creativity. Speak God's Word. Say, "God, I receive Your wisdom as my sister. Wisdom is by my side every single day!" Be persuaded that you will walk with confidence in every step you take as you welcome wisdom as your sidekick!

Receive all of God's wisdom cheerfully. Take comfort in the fact that His ways are far better than yours. Receive wisdom when she calls out to you; make her a comfortable place she can stay and dwell in, giving you direction and clarity. Ask for, depend on, and rely on wisdom. I pray that you call wisdom

Halene Giddens

your best friend and sister today. Allow her to take the lead in your life and be excessively blessed today!

Halene Giddens

S E V E N T E E N

He Knows All About Me

Every single moment you are thinking of me!
How precious and wonderful to consider
that you cherish me constantly in your every thought!
O God, your desires toward me are more
than the grains of sand on every shore!
When I awake each morning,
you're still with me.

Psalm 139:17-18 TPT

Dr. Halene Giddens

God bless you and praise the Lord! I pray that you are well, and as you go through your day, you seek to take time to rest in His presence; this is where He longs for you to be.

Psalm 139 is such a lovely and poetic song of awareness of God's constant presence with us. Knowing that the Almighty God in Heaven thinks about us every moment is unimaginable; it's incomprehensible. Yet, He does. Our Lord and Savior keeps us in His heart and His mind, and His thoughts toward us are always good. That's right! Every single thing that our Father thinks concerning His children is only good. He wants nothing more than for us to believe and trust in Him so we can live this good life.

This Psalm paints a picture of how God knows everything about us, how He reads our hearts like an open book, and knows every word we will speak. Verse five gives us an even greater understanding: He, with kindness, follows behind us to spare us

Halene Giddens

of the hurt and harm of our past! He's telling us we can let go and live life with the certainty that He knows all, is in all, and will bring us through all! He's even gone into our future and, this is good; He prepares the way for us.

He has thoroughly established in this Psalm that He knows everything about you. He has shown how He takes great care to let you see Him in everything, in all parts of your life. It is now your decision to let Him in completely. You can choose to give Him full access to everything concerning you. Give Him every part of your future as you let go and let Him have your past. He knows about it anyway.

Take the time to read Psalm 139 in its entirety. Let this love poem saturate your soul. I pray that as you realize the Father knows everything about you, He wants you to know everything about Him. He doesn't hide from you, and He won't turn away; you simply must trust that He is with you and will be right there when you call. "When I awake each morning, you're still with

Halene Giddens

me." He watches over you even as you sleep.

Be excessively blessed today as you dwell in His presence. Find out something new about the Father as you read His love letter to you. I love you!

Halene Giddens

E I G H T E E N

Receive the Freshness

Sharing in his death by our baptism
means that we were co-buried with him,
so that when the Father's glory
raised Christ from the dead,
we were also raised with him.
We have been co-resurrected with him
so that we could be empowered to walk
in the freshness of new life.

Romans 6:4 TPT

Dr. Halene Giddens

Hello! I pray you're doing well today. I pray you woke up with expectancy, looking forward to being refreshed in God's presence. Child of God, you have the opportunity to receive newness of life today just by spending time with the Lord.

Another way to say fresh is "up to date." When we determine to die to sin, as verse two tells us to do and let grace abound, we are walking in a new way; we've been updated. Another word for fresh is original. Isn't that beautiful! When we decide to walk with Christ, identifying with His death, burial, and resurrection, we are going back to our original state of purity and freshness! He made us in His image to be like Him; He longs to fellowship with us and to have a relationship with us every day. When we make the effort to bury our old way of thinking and doing things, along with letting go of our past mistakes, we have the opportunity to rise up with Him afresh and anew!

Halene Giddens

Be empowered to walk in the freshness of life today. Jesus' resurrection signifies and qualifies our new and fresh state. We can be invigorated with vitality daily when we are in constant communion with Him. God always intended for us to live our lives this way. Be intentional about your commitment to the Lord as you keep in mind the great sacrifice made for you to be free. You are a new creation in Christ. The old is gone; behold the new!

Receive the abundant life that Jesus came to give you. Walk in newness. Walk in freshness. Walk in all the beauty of what Christ did when He died on the cross. Bury the old you, arise in Him- new and full of power every single day! Have a wonderful day, and may God shower you with His abounding love and grace!

Halene Giddens

N I N E T E E N

David's Open Praise to God

Therefore David blessed the LORD before all the assembly;
and David said: "Blessed are You, LORD God of Israel, our Father,
forever and ever. Yours, O LORD, is the greatness, The power and the
glory, The victory and the majesty; For all that is in heaven and in
earth is Yours; Yours is the kingdom, O LORD, And You are exalted as
head over all. Both riches and honor come from You, And You reign over
all. In Your hand is power and might; In Your hand it is to make great
and to give strength to all. "Now therefore, our God, We thank You and
praise Your glorious name. But who am I, and who are my people,
That we should be able to offer so willingly as this? For all things come
from You, and of Your own we have given You.

I Chronicles 29:10-14 NKJV

Dr. Halene Giddens

I hope you are well today, and as you go through your routine, you would continually bless the Lord, acknowledge His Holy Spirit, and receive His Help. Today is a gift given to us by our Heavenly Father; it is specially made for you to take part and enjoy the beauty of this day. Rough times and challenging experiences are part of this journey, but I pray you would lift your head and find your ever-present Help in the midst of it all.

In these Scriptures in First Chronicles, David openly praises and glorifies God for the ability to give freely in such abundance to build God a sanctuary. David did not conceal his desire to build a Temple for the Lord where the people of God could worship and make sacrifices to their God.

David's closeness to God gave him the revelation that God is our Father. David is the first person in the Old Testament to call the Lord Father. Jesus introduced God as our Father in the New Testament and told us when He left that our Father would leave us with another Comforter, a Helper, and Guide: The Holy

Halene Giddens

Spirit. We still have this amazing Gift. He is the Holy Spirit, Who is right here with us always (John 14:16; 16:13). He is our inner Witness, leading and guiding us in the way we should go. He brings all things back to our remembrance that we need to know.

The prophet Joel in the Old Testament speaks of the Holy Spirit being poured out on all kinds of people: sons and daughters will prophesy, old men will dream dreams, and young men will see visions (Joel 2:28,29). Joel speaks of the Holy Spirit filling the people, foretelling the wondrous events in Acts.

David was sensitive to the Spirit of the Lord before the "outpouring" of the Holy Spirit was even given. He wrote songs and poems about the Spirit of the Lord being ever-present. The Holy Spirit is a Help to every person who receives Jesus Christ as their personal Lord and Savior. David recognized this in his lifetime. David envisioned what happened in Acts—the people of God coming together to worship the Lord, praying and

Halene Giddens

loving on Him. David perhaps knew then there was more to the assembling of God's people. The Holy Spirit was introduced to each individual in the Upper Room—the place where the people of God were assembled on the day of Pentecost! There's always something good about coming together as believers in Christ.

It's beautiful we can have a relationship with the Heavenly Father with the help of the Holy Spirit. We don't have to live this life in fear! We can, as David did, live a life blessing and praising our Lord's Holy and Majestic Name. We can gather with other believers and experience the manifestation of the Holy Spirit and receive His gifts for us poured out in and over our lives.

As you seek the Father, allow the Holy Spirit to be the Comforter and Guide in your personal life. Receive the power the disciples acquired; send up blessings and praise as David so freely and frequently did. Let the Holy Spirit live through you, not just in you. Be empowered with the help of the Holy Spirit and be excessively blessed!

Halene Giddens

TWENTY

We Have Help

And I will pray the Father,
and He will give you another Helper,
that He may abide with you forever —
the Spirit of truth,
whom the world cannot receive,
because it neither sees Him nor knows Him;
but you know Him,
for He dwells with you and will be in you.

John 14:16-17 NKJV

Dr. Halene Giddens

God bless you today! I pray you woke up inviting the Holy Spirit to be with you and embrace His ministry in your life today. One of the beautiful parts about the Holy Spirit is that you can receive His Ministry for your benefit regardless of your race, age, background, political or social affiliation. Having Jesus Christ is your key to receiving the Holy Spirit as your personal concierge, or a better term is your Aid Ally and Personal Companion!

We have this beautiful gift of the Holy Spirit because Jesus promised that our Father would leave us with a Comforter: another Person in the Trinity Who loves us and cares for us. Jesus promised we wouldn't be left alone to fend for ourselves. If we receive the Holy Spirit, He will help us and guide us. If we employ the Holy Spirit, He will appease our troubled minds and weary hearts.

Just like the disciples on the day of Pentecost, we can anticipate the promise of His power infiltrating our lives, causing

Halene Giddens

this life we live to be fulfilling! We can call on Abba Father to be with us every moment of every day because of the Holy Spirit's ministry in operation! We can stay the course today with the Holy Spirit's help.

There are so many benefits to receiving the Holy Spirit's guidance every day; all we have to do is ask Him, which means acknowledging Him. Invite Him in your every moment, and He'll be right there with you. He is listening to you, keeping you, leading you in what to say, how to pray, what to do, and when to do it! Although the Holy Spirit's ministry has always been working and moving in the earth, He was not poured out on God's people in the same manner He was in the book of Acts--the way He is now, the way He can be with you. So, you and I can connect with the Holy Spirit right now. Under the old covenant found in the Old Testament, the people of God had Him on occasion. But every time we speak and even breathe, He can be right there!

Halene Giddens

Allow the gift of the Holy Spirit to lead and empower you. Let Him use His full ministry through you when He desires to. Call Him your loving, caring, sharing, Heavenly Father. Put a smile on His face today as you trust your life to Him. Have a wonderfully, excessively blessed day! I pray you remain in the place of peace as you focus on the Father.

Halene Giddens

Pause in His Presence

TWENTY-ONE

Our Great Hope

*And I heard a loud voice from heaven saying,
"Behold, the tabernacle of God is with men,
and He will dwell with them,
and they shall be His people.
God Himself will be with them
and be their God."*

Revelations 21:3 KJV

Dr. Halene Giddens

I pray you are doing well and that you are basking in God's peace and grace. He is pleased when we delight ourselves in Him. So, be captivated in His presence and allow Him to respond to your prayers today.

As sons and daughters of God, we know our position and place in Him is sealed; we are His. What a wonderful promise we have to hold onto. Let's take this knowledge and pray for our loved ones, friends, neighbors, and anyone who does not have a personal relationship with the Father.

The Book of Revelations speaks of the judgment and justice that will come to those who refuse the Father's invitation. Nevertheless, we are the ones who can bring people the hope that they can live their lives on this side of Heaven with God as our help. He promised that just as He is right here with us now in the person of the Holy Spirit, He will dwell with us in the new Heaven and new earth.

Halene Giddens

Though the judgment is imminent, it does not have to be feared. God promised all who are sealed with the Holy Spirit a place in Heaven with Him. Let's pray for those who do not know; let's lead them by not only our talk but also by our walk with Him. Let others see that we are His because our lives are a bright light in this dark world. Let's be a witness of His grace, goodness, love, kindness, and mercy. Let's allow ourselves to be the conduit of God's graciousness here on the earth!

We can look forward to the day that we will dwell in His presence in the new earth. We will see Him Face to face for Who He is! Right now, He lives in you by His Spirit! We have this blessed assurance; we can reside with Him right now in our human existence and in that new place of Glory! Be in faith today. God bless you!

Halene Giddens

TWENTY-TWO

The Secret Place

He that dwelleth in the secret place
of the Most High Shall abide
under the shadow of the Almighty.

Psalm 91:1 KJV

He who dwells in the shelter
of the Most High
will remain secure and rest
in the shadow of the Almighty
[whose power no enemy can withstand].
I will say of the Lord,
"He is my refuge and my fortress,
My God, in whom I trust
[with great confidence, and on whom I rely]!"

Psalm 91:1-2 AMP

Dr. Halene Giddens

I pray you are doing well today and are refreshed knowing that your God is with you; just invite Him into your space, into your thoughts, and into your heart. He is always just a moment away; dwell in the comfort of His presence today.

Psalm 91 is God's Canopy of Protection over His people. God is our Vigilant Protector, a Secret Place for those who choose to come to Him for safety. We can abide in His shadow, which is always a cool and refreshing place, a hiding place from catastrophe. This Psalm describes in great detail all that God can be for us if we enter into His presence.

This illustration of God shows Him as our Armor, One Who protects us from those things that seek to overwhelm, devastate, and cause us great peril! Being in Him means we do not have to fear whatever may come our way. We are safe and secure when we step into this secret place, which is only a thought away. The Psalm goes on further to say all that we can do and have access to when we stay close to Him. We can walk all over every

Halene Giddens

demonic attack of the wicked. No matter the significance of the spiritual, mental, or physical attack coming against you, you can walk on top of it! That's the promise of God's protection! We have angels watching over us, continually keeping us in all that we do.

Then our Father begins to speak to us, promising that He will snatch us away from the adverse effects of destruction and set us on a pinnacle, the highest place of honor because we know His Name. He will lift us to where He is if we allow Him to. There is no better place than above our circumstances, challenges, and constant demands. He will answer us when we call on Him.

In this life, we're going to experience heartache and pain. There is no safer place in these times than in our Father's shadow in the secret place. When we choose to stay in the secret place-- the safe place, the place of shelter-- we are kept and covered on every side.

Halene Giddens

Know you have access to a fortress, an encampment of protection from every device of the enemy. Trust your life with Him and hideaway in His secret place. He is covering you with His strong and mighty wings; He will take care of you; He will guard you against all hurt, harm, and danger. Continue to confess and declare God's Canopy of Protection over your life and the lives of your loved ones, family, and friends. Trust that God's Canopy is a reliant force against every foe. Be excessively blessed today!

Halene Giddens

TWENTY-THREE

Receive The Holy Spirit's Help

*And when the day of Pentecost was fully come,
they were all with one accord in one place.
And suddenly there came a sound from heaven
as of a rushing mighty wind,
and it filled all the house where they were sitting.*

Acts 2:1-2 KJV

Dr. Halene Giddens

I pray you are well today! I hope you have entered into the presence of the Lord through prayer, praise, along with worship. Open up your heart's door to the Lord, allow Him to whisper in your ear so that you may hear all that He has for you today.

The Apostles turned the world upside down with their radical belief in Jesus Christ, accepting Him as the Way, the Truth, and the Life and living their lives to spread the Gospel worldwide. They turned the world right-side up with their Holy Ghost-filled fiery messages about the Messiah and His imminent return!

They believed the Comforter would come; Jesus told them He would! They received the Holy Spirit, allowing Him to take His place in their hearts and minds. They may not have fully understood all that the Holy Spirit was meant to be to them, but they trusted Jesus when He told them to receive this power from on high! We can trust our Savior and Lord! We can make the same choice, receive this Precious Gift of the Holy Spirit and allow Him to take the lead in our lives today!

Halene Giddens

The Apostles and others were gathered together in an upper room. The outside world assailed them with thoughts of suffering the same fate as their Master. These thoughts and emotions would be daunting without the overcoming power of the Holy Spirit! Then the Holy Ghost came upon them in their gathering place. This fire, this power not only transformed them individually, but with the help of the Holy Ghost, they went out and changed the lives of people around them, their communities, the nations, and the world. It didn't matter the trial or tribulation; they persevered because of their strong belief and everlasting hope in the Message. Nothing was the same once they received the power of the Holy Spirit.

This same confidence can be with you. You have the Message in your heart. Jesus' words of hope, love, and truth are yours to spread and share with those around you. Allow the Holy Spirit to stir your heart, mind, and soul to spread the Gospel to all those who want to receive Him. The Holy Spirit came to take away all fear, so we can be full of faith and determined to fulfill

Halene Giddens

our God-given assignment!

Let His love fill you with compassion for all His people He wants to bring to salvation. Jesus came to give us an abundant life, a life lived in the presence and with the power of His Holy Spirit so that we can live empowered for our purpose on this side of heaven!

With this power of love and a sound mind, be radical for Christ, just as the Apostles were. Let the Holy Spirit come up out of you because He is already in you. You've got access to the free gift given to all His people right on the inside of you! Like the early Apostles, go out and change not just your world but the world around you. Pause in His presence. Dwell in His presence, live in His presence, find strength in His Presence. Allow the Holy Spirit to shine through you and share the Good News of Jesus Christ. God bless you today as you abide in His ever-abundant glorious presence!

Halene Giddens

T W E N T Y - F O U R

David's Poetic Praise to God!

Yahweh is my best friend and my shepherd.
I always have more than enough.
He offers a resting place for me in his luxurious love.
His tracks take me to an oasis of peace near the quiet brook of bliss.
That's where he restores and revives my life.
He opens before me the right path and leads me along in his footsteps
of righteousness so that I can bring honor to his name.

Psalm 23:1-3 TPT

Dr. Halene Giddens

I pray you welcome this day with praises and prayers to the Almighty God. He is the Only One worthy of worship, adoration, and thanksgiving. He keeps every promise and never leaves us alone; His love endures forever, and His mercies are new every morning. Therefore, embrace this day because He made you for this very moment. Keep the mind of Christ, keep His Word near, meditate on His Word, apply it to your life, and allow situations in your life to change for the better.

Psalm 23, one of the most infamous passages of Scripture, is written by King David. This warrior was a worshipper first and readily changed from his kingly robes to the priestly garments. Like David, we can transition in our lives, receiving a separate anointing, a special grace for a specific purpose. Before going into any spiritual war or battle, worship must precede us. Remember, our warfare is spiritual; we're not fighting against the flesh (Ephesians 6:12). David spent a lot of time at war, but worship was always his focus.

David's revelation of God's unconditional love for him made

Halene Giddens

worship a necessity in his life. Worship was essential to David. He realized his intimate relationship with God was everything; it was the only thing that kept his heart and mind through the difficult times in his life. David recognized God as his Father and Good Shepherd, keeping and leading him through every battle He faced. His personal relationship with the Lord allowed him to be led in every victory he received.

In this Psalm, David encourages us that the comfort of God's love takes away fear. God gives more than enough. Allow Him to calm your heart and rest your mind. Allow Him to bless you excessively right in the middle of enemy territory! Allow the Holy Spirit to guide your thoughts. Build a personal relationship with the Heavenly Father, one that sustains you through every storm. Like David, let Yahweh become your Best Friend and live out the benefits of your salvation through your worship experience. Let God's hand lead you as He loves you through every crisis. Let Him be the Good Shepherd over your life.

Halene Giddens

He wants to be that Best Friend that you constantly hang out with. He longs to have a real and meaningful connection with you. Choose to put worship before everything you do and trust that you will always have more than enough with His guidance. Take that break in God's presence, continually allowing Him to lead you to peaceful encounters with Him. Be excessively blessed!

Halene Giddens

T W E N T Y - F I V E

God's Love Is For All

But those who hope in the Lord
will be happy and pleased!
Our help comes from the God of Jacob!
You open the eyes of the blind,
and you fully restore those bent over with shame.
You love those who love and honor you.

Psalm 146:5&8 TPT

Dr. Halene Giddens

I pray you are well today and that you are keeping your eyes lifted up to Heaven no matter what is going on around you. Lift your heart as you lift your head with your prayers to God the Father. He hears you and comforts you in every circumstance. He truly is a Good Father and loves when His children come to Him to spend time in His presence, conversing and listening to Him.

We can often put so much into what man says--their promises, agendas, and even their wealth. God has given us leaders, and we are to pray for them and keep them uplifted, but they are not to take God's place in our hearts. Instead, God has called us to be set apart and look to Him for help.

Beloved saint of the Most High God, I pray as we face hard issues in this life, some more uncomfortable than others, that we meet them with the Word of God and the Heart of God as our focus. God is not prejudiced, and He gives His loving kindness equally to anyone and everyone willing to receive it. As believers, we should

Halene Giddens

be concerned with all matters, even if they make us uncomfortable, because God cares for all people and shows no partiality. If we value and love others that do not look, talk, or act like us, we must want His heart and be sensitive to the Spirit's leading to show kindness to all kinds of people.

The Lord is the One Who examines our hearts, so allow Him to keep your heart protected from judgment and harm. Listen to the heartbeat of the Father and to what He is speaking into your life today. Let your eyes be opened and not blinded by the concerns of your current situation.

I pray you are comforted by God's Word and continue to find your strength in Christ. He is our only hope and reward. Give your attention to honoring Him in all that you do. Make it your priority today to show those who are spiritually blind or bent over with shame that there is a love that restores and a Spirit that heals. Be that conduit of God's love and graciousness. Stay connected to Him today, and may your hope in Him put a smile on His face!

Halene Giddens

Pause in His Presence

T W E N T Y - S I X

God's Destiny Fulfilled!

*We have become his poetry, a re-created people
that will fulfill the destiny he has given each of us,
for we are joined to Jesus, the Anointed One.
Even before we were born, God planned in advance
our destiny and the good works we would do to fulfill it!*

Ephesians 2:10 TPT

Dr. Halene Giddens

I pray you are excessively blessed today! I pray you are resting in the authority and power He's placed on the inside of you. You have been in God's plan since before the earth was created. Therefore, you can live your life in expectation that you have a predetermined destiny God has already mapped out for you.

We are created in His image; fearfully and wonderfully, He made us in our mother's womb. That means He's made you and me to be awesome! He created us on purpose for His purpose to be a part of His glorious worldwide plan! He ingrafted us into the beauty of His family. Each one of us is in the magnanimous family of the Living God! That's pretty great news! In the vastness of the body of Christ, He knows our name; He even knows the number of hairs on our heads; each follicle has its own number! Can you imagine the immense pride God takes in you to give each hair on your head a number! He cares for you more than you can comprehend! God, our Heavenly Father, wants to have an intimate personal relationship with us; He wants to be

Halene Giddens

our Friend. It is no accident that we are here at this precise time. By His great divine design, we are placed at this moment to be a bearer of His grace and love.

We are each called; we all have a purpose. If we join our lives with Him, we can do all He has formed and fashioned us to do. There is an advance directive on our lives. We know advance directives to be used in the medical field, and in this verse, God is telling us that He's given us written instructions in which way we are to live our lives. He gives us His Word, His Spirit, and His preachers so we can successfully carry out all He has designed us to do. There are no secrets with Him. We should live our lives ready to carry out His divine will.

This chapter in the book of Ephesians encourages us that we have direct access into the realm of the Holy Spirit to come before the Father (verse 18). This realm is His presence. As children of God, we have power, authority, and full access to Him. Remember, He's only a thought away. So, let's walk in the

Halene Giddens

purpose He has called us to.

Give your life entirely over to the Father. Let Him work out the destiny He put inside of you. Dwell in His presence daily and walk in the confidence that He has predestined for you. He will give you the grace, wisdom, and peace needed to fulfill your destiny. God bless you, and may you be lifted up above the fray and over every foe to fulfill His Will in your life!

Halene Giddens

T W E N T Y - S E V E N

Overwhelmed in His Presence

*Whenever my busy thoughts were out of control,
the soothing comfort of your presence
calmed me down and overwhelmed me with delight.*

Psalm 94:19 TPT

Dr. Halene Giddens

Praise the Lord to Him be all the glory, dominion, and praise! I pray you are rejoicing in this day, that you are happy to be among the living once again because He still has so much more in store for you. Therefore, delight yourself in Him and give your cares over to Him as He longs to give you answers of peace and hope.

Psalm 94 in the Passion Translation is entitled "God of Vengeance." When you read the entire chapter, you hear David's heart and transparency about how God does not take it lightly when the wicked treat God's children with evilness. David had many first-hand encounters in battle, going to war with those who were against his God. Therefore, he spoke from experience about God's protection and His promise of safety. David knew God as a fortress from those who meant him harm.

Yet, in this pericope, David inserted verse 19. It's as though he recognized another enemy outside of those we see in this physical and natural realm, which is not always evident. That

Halene Giddens

enemy can, at times, be the "inner me." David had to address this subtle adversary that can, in his words, get "out of control."

The outside world can be loud, invasive, and maddening, causing anger, malice, and hatred. We must be mindful and careful that these outer disturbances do not cause us to be distracted and abandon our faith in our Father's protection and love. Besides the outer noise, the inner turmoil of our minds can be a constant struggle that we may find challenging to overcome. Our thoughts can be worrisome and busy with things that are out of our control. We constantly must boldly speak the word of God, not allowing these thoughts to take over or deter us from His amazing path and plan for us! He is our first line of defense against the assailing thoughts in our minds.

The beauty of David's revelation is that we can shift our thoughts from a place of overwhelming distress to a place of calm in His presence where there is immediate comfort and peace. We can become overwhelmed with delight! Just as we

Halene Giddens

trust our Father to shield us against the enemy in this world, He will also be a guard around the thoughts that can lead to anxiety, depression, mental stress, and sickness. We simply must come to our Heavenly Father and allow Him to be right there with us in those anxious moments.

You can't always control the anxious and stressful thoughts that try to overwhelm you, but you can call out to your God right in the middle of all that mental and emotional activity. Child of God, I pray you understand you are only one thought away from being in the Father's presence where you can experience peace when thoughts become busy and out of control. He wants to provide you with the solace and comfort you need for your heart and mind; you only need to ask. May you find yourself in His presence today, allowing your thoughts to become calm, soothing your mind from all apprehension, tension, and stress. God bless you!

Halene Giddens

TWENTY-EIGHT

You Will Flourish!

But the godly will flourish like palm trees
and grow strong like the cedars of Lebanon.
For they are transplanted to the Lord's own house.
They flourish in the courts of our God.
Even in old age they will still produce fruit;
they will remain vital and green.

Psalm 92:12-14 NLT

Dr. Halene Giddens

God bless you today! It is a wonderful day to be alive with the ability to give praise to our King for placing us right where we belong in His presence. I pray you find restoration and peace right now as you take the time to abide in the Strong Fortress of His arms.

The book of Psalms is filled with many poetic songs of praise, worship, thanksgiving, as well as heartfelt thoughts, meditations, and even expressions of great anguish, all directed to our God. I'm so grateful that these poets and psalmists recounted their devotion to the Lord along with their inner struggles and great triumphs for our benefit! This allows us to encounter their relationship with the Lord and motivates us to develop our worship and devotion to the Most High God. The book of Psalms gives us a glimpse of their expressive heart cries to their God. Their open concerns and quandaries, coupled with their desire to be faithful to the Almighty, are an inspiration to all who take the time to enjoy them.

Halene Giddens

Psalm 92 reminds us that as we continue to live out our years in service to our God, we can flourish in all that we endeavor to do. This word flourish in the Hebrew Translation means to bloom, to abundantly blossom, to spring up, to break forth, and to figuratively spread your wings. Yes, as we walk out our days loving and living for our God, we can still blossom, bloom, and grow! When we are planted in the Lord's House (that simply means connecting to a local assembly of believers that follows the teachings of Christ), we can accomplish so many amazing things for God's Kingdom.

We are transplanted from the world's way of thinking and doing into the House of our God. We have the advantage of no longer following after those things that cause us harm and set us back from living a fruit-filled life. The renewing of our mind now transforms us, daily allowing the Holy Spirit to lead and guide us in our decision making, living, and giving.

Now that we are no longer the same, we can continually

Halene Giddens

grow strong. As we seek the Lord's Presence, which He freely gives us access to, we flourish in every area of our lives. As we pursue Him, we will thrive and prosper even in our old age.

Be encouraged today to set yourself aside to be with the Lord. Stay in the Lord's own house and be determined to flourish in His courts. Abundance is exactly what God has for you! Your labor in and outside the House of God matters and can make an impact in your community. He desires that you bear fruit that will benefit you in your life and affect the lives of others around you. Stay in His presence, discover what areas of your life God desires for you to flourish in, and be excessively blessed! Flourish in all that God has called and gifted you to be; you are made to bear fruit that will last forever.

Halene Giddens

T W E N T Y - N I N E

Who Comes Before the King?

Those who are clean —
whose works and ways are pure,
whose hearts are true and sealed by the truth,
those who never deceive, whose words are sure.
They will receive Yahweh's blessing
and righteousness given by the Savior-God.
They will stand before God,
for they seek the pleasure of God's face,
the God of Jacob. Pause in his presence

Psalm 24:4-6 TPT

Dr. Halene Giddens

God bless you! I pray you are excessively blessed today. I pray that right now, you take a moment to breathe and simply be in God's presence. Worship Him right where you are. Invite Him into your home, workplace, and school; wherever you are right now, invite Him in. Take this minute to bless the Name of the Lord Most High.

Psalm 24 has three short divisions, and this second division is called "Who Comes Before the King?" As you take this time to just be in His company, allow your heart to be lifted up. Take inventory of your thoughts, words, actions, and stance with Him. It's so easy to forget that He sees all we do; everything that comes from our lips, along with the meditations of our hearts, are heard by Him. Bring the Lord to your thoughts, all that He means to you, and how He is your first Love. Commit once more to allow Him to be in the forefront of all that you do; in every thought, make Him the center and circumference.

Halene Giddens

You can stay right in this place, right in this moment, when you continue to meditate on His goodness and His grace. You can stay here as you remind Him and yourself how grateful you are for Him being the King over your life. No matter what is on your agenda for the rest of the day, no matter what you planned for the future, you can stay in this place of peace, rest, and comfort.

Now that you have entered in, now that you have paused in His presence, let the Holy Spirit lead you and guide you today. You have victory in every situation as you allow Him to govern your life. He reigns on high and wants you to stay in the realm where you know for certain He provides all you could ever want or need. So, as you set your heart to give adoration to the King forever, be abundantly blessed. In Jesus' Holy Name, Amen!

Halene Giddens

T H I R T Y

Keep Him in Remembrance

*Then they that feared the Lord
spake often one to another:
and the Lord hearkened, and heard it,
and a book of remembrance
was written before him for them
that feared the Lord,
and that thought upon his name.
And they shall be mine, saith the Lord of hosts,
in that day when I make up my jewels;
and I will spare them, as a man spareth
his own son that serveth him.*

Malachi 3:16-17 KJV

Halene Giddens

I pray you are doing well today and all is going your way in the Lord as you walk with Him. Wherever you are right now, I pray that you take this time to recognize that He is with you and wants to commune with you.

The third chapter of Malachi is famously known for verses eight through ten, where the prophet encourages us in our giving, but I'd like to point out two other verses of scripture in this chapter. Malachi reminds us in verse 16 that the Lord hears those who fear Him. In the New Living Translation, it reads: "In His presence, a scroll of remembrance was written to record the names of those who feared Him and always thought about the honor of His name." Our names are written in His presence! Isn't this beautiful, child of God?

Malachi says in verse 17 that we belong to the Lord, and we are His jewels. Oh, how His Word is filled with such amazing blessings. What a beautiful promise: we are His special treasure! Those of us that speak of the Lord and talk about Him one with

Halene Giddens

another will be remembered. Malachi is the last book in the Old Testament, and it's as though the Lord wanted His people to remember that He Sees and Hears them, and He will always continue to do so! It's as though the Lord wanted His precious people to keep speaking of His goodness, remembering and reminding themselves of all He had brought them through. It would be 400 years before the book of Matthew.

Beloved, meditate on the Word of God. Speak of Him often to fellow Believers. Never let a single day go by when we do not remember His promises and all He has done to prove His love. He is committed to remembering us; our names are written in a scroll and remain in His presence. Therefore, make it your pledge to write His name on the tablet of your heart and stay in His presence. I love you and pray that you choose to be excessively blessed!

Halene Giddens

THIRTY-ONE

Freedom in His Presence

Looking around, she replied,
"I see no one, Lord."
Jesus said, "Then I certainly
don't condemn you either.
Go, and from now on,
be free from a life of sin."

John 8:11 TPT

Dr. Halene Giddens

God bless you! This is such a beautiful day to be alive, and I hope you are experiencing every joy and pleasure in Him as you go about completing your tasks today. It's in Him we live, move, and have our being, so let's enter into His presence and stay right there.

The beginning of John chapter eight is a very familiar passage where the religious leaders and Pharisees brought to Jesus a woman caught in the very act of adultery. Can you believe it? The very act! And where exactly was the man? Adultery does take at least two people!

How clever they must have thought they were, using this woman as bait to catch the Master Creator in some sort of religious trap! Would Jesus condemn the woman to death by stoning as the law of Moses commanded, or would He condemn the law, allowing her to go free and, thereby, igniting fury from the religious leaders?

Halene Giddens

After their persistence for an answer of what should be done to the woman, Jesus paused for a few moments and then answered, "Let's have the man who has never had a sinful desire throw the first stone at her."

Silence.

"Until finally, Jesus was left alone with the woman still standing there in front of Him."

No matter what you have done, where you have been, or who you have been with, I encourage you to come to your moment where you are alone with Jesus. Regardless of our sin issues, past or present, each of us has fallen short of the glory of God. No matter who may try to condemn you, Jesus declares your freedom today! So don't condemn yourself. Receive your Liberty! For whom the Son sets free is free indeed!

The beauty is this: He does not condemn you. Remember

Halene Giddens

this as you continue to walk out this journey and know that this privilege comes with no strings attached. Be alone with Him and discover the freedom He gives as often as you need to be reminded of it. He gave His life for you to be free today, so celebrate this independence from sin. Be free in your mind and emotions. Moreover, be free from the curse of sin, death, hell, and the grave. He has redeemed you. Find yourself alone often with Him and embrace the freedom He chose to give. God bless you today!

Halene Giddens

Made in the USA
Columbia, SC
23 September 2021